S0-AHS-245

9321
HARRIS COUNTY PUBLIC LIBRARY

What Makes Me Stinky?

By Wes Flynn

Gareth Stevens
Publishing

Please visit our website, www.garethstevens.com. For a free color catalog of all our high-quality books, call toll free 1-800-542-2595 or fax 1-877-542-2596.

Library of Congress Cataloging-in-Publication Data

Flynn, Wes.
What makes me stinky? / by Wes Flynn.
  p. cm. — (My body does strange stuff!)
Includes index.
ISBN 978-1-4824-0304-6 (pbk.)
ISBN 978-1-4824-0305-3 (6-pack)
ISBN 978-1-4824-0301-5 (library binding)
1. Body odor — Juvenile literature. 2. Hygiene — Juvenile literature. I. Title.
RA780.F59 2014
613—dc23

Published in 2014 by
Gareth Stevens Publishing
111 East 14th Street, Suite 349
New York, NY 10003

Designer: Michael J. Flynn
Editor: Greg Roza

Photo credits: Cover, p. 1 altrendo images/Altrendo/Getty Images; p. 5 Yellow Dog Productions/Lifesize/Getty Images; p. 7 Fotokostic/Shutterstock.com; p. 9 White Packert/The Image Bank/Getty Images; p. 11 Horst Petzold/Shutterstock.com; p. 12 Pete Pahham/Shutterstock.com; p. 15 Jorg Hackemann/Shutterstock.com; p. 17 Westend61/Getty Images; p. 19 Elena Elisseeva/Shutterstock.com; p. 21 Dmitry Meinikov/Shutterstock.com.

Contents

Boldface words appear in the glossary.

I Stink!

You may have stinky breath when you wake up in the morning. You **sweat** and get stinky when playing kickball. Your feet may stink when you take off your shoes after the game. What makes all these bad **odors**? Read on to find out!

Everyday Dirty

The more active you are, the dirtier you probably get, even if you can't see the dirt! You might get dirty playing outside, but you may also get sweaty. The dirt, sweat, and other things that get on your body can make you stink.

No Sweat!

Sweating happens when we're hot, when we exercise, and when we play with our friends. For most people, sweating often leads to body odor. However, sweat usually has no smell. Body odor is caused by tiny **creatures** that live on skin and eat sweat!

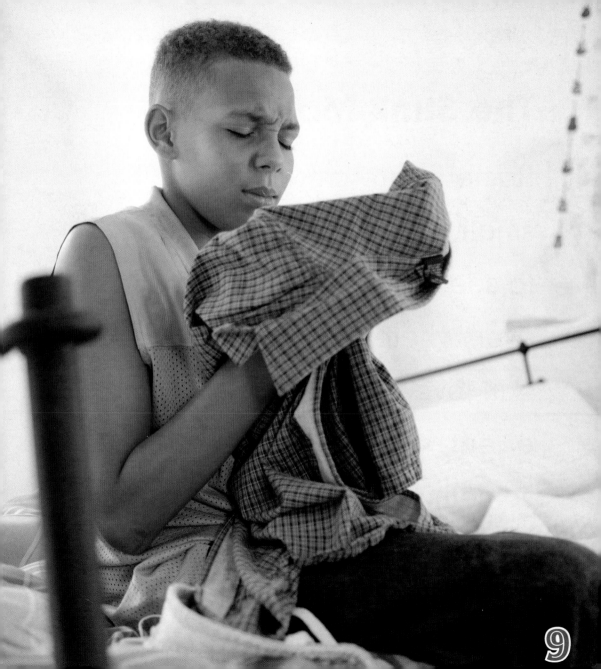

The Stink Makers

Bacteria are creatures so small we need a **microscope** to see them. They live almost everywhere. The bacteria on your skin love sweat. They consume, or eat, sweat and change it into something different. This is what makes sweat smell bad.

11

Sweat is mostly water and a little salt. Strong emotions may cause the body to make another kind of sweat. This kind may have an odor, but it doesn't usually smell bad. However, this is the kind of sweat bacteria love to eat.

SWEAT GLANDS

A gland is a body part that makes something the body needs. There are two kinds of sweat glands.

eccrine glands

- located all over the body
- make sweat that is mostly water and a little salt
- make sweat that helps cool off the body when it's hot

apocrine glands

- located mainly in skin that has hair
- make sweat that contains water, salt, fat, and oils
- make sweat because of stress and strong emotions
- become active as our body changes when we become adults
- when bacteria break down or consume apocrine sweat, bad odors are produced

Too Much Sweat

Some people sweat more than others. This means they can stink more than other people. **Excessive** sweating can lead to body odor, but it can also be a sign of a bigger problem. If you sweat for no reason, it's a good idea to go see a doctor.

15

Dark and Damp

Different types of bacteria live on different parts of the body. These different bacteria can make different odors, but they all smell bad. Bacteria love dark, damp areas. This is why your feet really stink after a long day in your sneakers. Yuck!

17

Don't Forget to Brush

Believe it or not, bacteria live in your mouth, too! They eat bits of food and create bad odors. Some food, such as onions or fish, also cause bad breath. The best way to get rid of bad breath is to brush your teeth in the morning and after eating.

19

Time to Come Clean

Soap and water will get rid of most bad odors. It's also important to wash your clothes often. However, if you have trouble getting rid of a bad smell, you may have a larger problem. You may want to ask a doctor.

21

Glossary

creature: an animal

excessive: more than normal, or more than enough

microscope: a tool used to make very tiny things look bigger

odor: a smell

sweat: liquid made by the skin and released to help cool off the body when it's hot. Also, to produce sweat.

For More Information

Books

Barnhill, Kelly Regan. *The Sweaty Book of Sweat.* Mankato, MN: Capstone Press, 2010.

James, Lincoln. *What Happens When I Sweat?* New York, NY: Gareth Stevens, 2014.

Kenah, Katharine. *Fascinating! Human Bodies.* Greensboro, NC: Spectrum, 2013.

Websites

What's Sweat?
kidshealth.org/kid/talk/yucky/sweat.html
Read more about sweat and why it makes us stink.

Why Do Feet Stink?
kidshealth.org/kid/talk/yucky/feet_stink.html
Learn more about the bacteria that cause stinky feet.

Publisher's note to educators and parents: Our editors have carefully reviewed these websites to ensure that they are suitable for students. Many websites change frequently, however, and we cannot guarantee that a site's future contents will continue to meet our high standards of quality and educational value. Be advised that students should be closely supervised whenever they access the Internet.

Index